PROFILES

Bob Marley
Chris May

Illustrated by
Trevor Parkin

Evans Brothers Limited

Published by Evans Brothers Limited
2A Portman Mansions
Chiltern Street
London W1M 1LE

First published in Great Britain in 1985 by
Hamish Hamilton Children's Books

© Chris May (text) 1985

© Trevor Parkin (illustrations) 1985

All Rights Reserved. No part of this publication may
be reproduced, stored in a retrieval system or
transmitted in any form or by any means, electronic,
mechanical, photocopying, recording or otherwise,
without prior permission of Evans Brothers Limited.

Reprinted in 1987, 1992

Typeset by Pioneer
Printed by Stephens & George Ltd,
   South Wales, Great Britain.
   Tel: 0685 5351

ISBN 0 237 60017 X

Titles in this series

Ian Botham	0 237 60030 7	Bob Geldof	0 237 60031 5
Edith Cavell	0 237 60020 X	Amy Johnson	0 237 60032 3
Marie Curie	0 237 60024 2	Helen Keller	0 237 60016 1
Roald Dahl	0 237 60010 2	John F. Kennedy	0 237 60029 3
Thomas Edison	0 237 60006 4	Florence Nightingale	0 237 60018 8
Alexander Fleming	0 237 60013 7	Emmeline Pankhurst	0 237 60019 6
John Lennon	0 237 60021 8	Anna Pavlova	0 237 60002 1
Martin Luther King	0 237 60007 2	Pope John Paul II	0 237 60005 6
Nelson Mandela	0 237 60026 9	Prince Philip	0 237 60012 9
Bob Marley	0 237 60017 X	Queen Elizabeth II	0 237 60302 0
Mother Teresa	0 237 60008 0	Queen Elizabeth the	
Margot Fonteyn	0 237 60033 1	Queen Mother	0 237 60009 9
Anne Frank	0 237 60015 3	Queen Victoria	0 237 60001 3
Elizabeth Fry	0 237 60028 5	Viv Richards	0 237 60027 7
Gandhi	0 237 60011 0	Margaret Thatcher	0 237 60003 X
Indira Gandhi	0 237 60025 0		

Contents

1	POSITIVE VIBRATION	9
2	COUNTRY BOY	12
3	CONCRETE JUNGLE	16
4	THE BIRTH OF THE WAILERS	20
5	REBEL MUSIC	26
6	RASTA MAN CHANT	30
7	CATCH A FIRE	34
8	ROOTS AND BRANCHES	39
9	SO MUCH TROUBLE IN THE WORLD	42
10	EXODUS	50

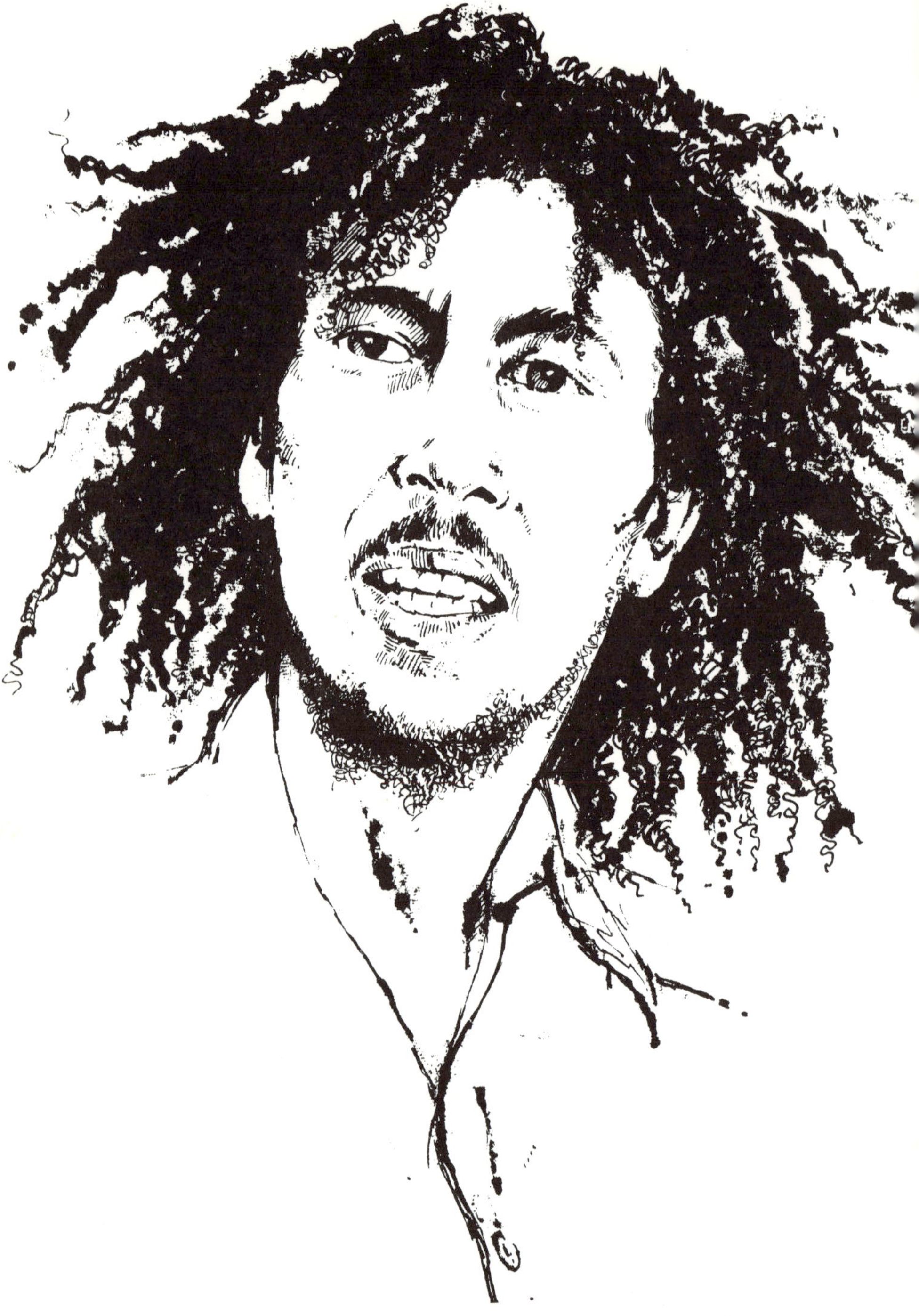

1 Positive Vibration

On 8 May 1984, *Island Records* released their twelfth album by Bob Marley and the Wailers. Titled Legend, *Island* were expecting the album to sell quickly and in large numbers, like all the other records that Bob had made since joining the label in 1972. But even *Island* were left breathless by the sheer size of the success of Legend. Within one week of the album's release it had reached number one in the British charts, selling an incredible 300,000 copies. Six weeks later Legend was still at number one, having now sold no less than 600,000 copies. This was in Britain alone. In America, Japan, Jamaica, Africa and all over Europe, it was enjoying a similar success. It was the fastest and biggest-selling album in the history of *Island*.

All this would have been remarkable enough had Bob been alive. But in 1984 he had been dead for three years. Even so, he could still sell more records than any other pop star, including those who were able to give concert tours promoting their latest releases. Only one other pop star could rival him in terms of runaway international success, and that was the phenomenally popular Michael Jackson.

The rise of Bob Marley in the intensely competitive pop world is a fascinating story in itself; it is a doubly fascinating story when you consider that Bob came from a tiny island in the Caribbean sea — Jamaica — which had never before produced a pop star who had made any sort of impact beyond its own shores. While Britain, for instance, has a population of some fifty-two million people, Jamaica has only around two-and-a-half million. For such a small country to produce a world star like Bob really is a very special achievement.

*   *   *

Jamaica first came to the attention of Europeans in 1494, when the explorer Christopher Columbus landed on the island. At that time Jamaica was populated by the Arawak Indians, but they were soon outnumbered

Christopher Columbus arriving in Jamaica

by the slaves who began arriving after 1500. The Spanish employers of Christopher Columbus, and the British who captured the island from them in 1655, enslaved hundreds of thousands of Africans to work on the sugar and banana plantations. In 1833 Britain outlawed slavery, but this made little real difference to the lives of most black people in Jamaica, who continued to live in poverty and hunger despite being officially 'free'. A proud and hard-working people, black Jamaicans have never forgotten how they first arrived in their new country, and their music and art have always included a large proportion of protest works and messages. The music Bob chose to play, called 'reggae', was part of this tradition of protest, with songs attacking slavery and the continuing oppression of black Jamaicans.

A relatively recent development, reggae first emerged towards the end of the 1960s, growing out of earlier Jamaican styles known as 'ska' and 'rocksteady'. All these styles have their roots in various forms of folk music which originally came with the slaves from Africa. When Bob first began making records in the 1960s, reggae was only just beginning to evolve, and record companies in Europe and America regarded it as a strictly local style which would never sell in their own countries. Yet within fifteen years, Bob had almost single-handedly turned the music into one of the most popular the world had ever known. Just how he did this, in the face of tremendous obstacles and prejudices, is the amazing story which will be explored in the chapters that follow.

2 Country Boy

When Bob was an adult, leading the Wailers and selling records all over the world, many of the songs that made him famous were about the lives of poor people living in the slums in Jamaica's capital city, Kingston. Songs like Concrete Jungle, Trenchtown Rock, and Burnin' And Lootin' described the terrible conditions that so many working-class Jamaicans had to endure (and still have to endure today). Bob grew to know the Kingston slums well when he was a teenager, so he was writing these songs from first-hand experience.

However, Bob was actually born in a beautiful country area of Jamaica known as the parish of St Ann (just as Britain is divided up into counties, so Jamaica is split into parishes). Known locally as 'the garden parish', St Ann is situated along the north coast of Jamaica, with wonderful beaches, cool sea breezes and a fertile soil which produces rich crops of coconuts, bananas, sugar and coffee. A nicer place to grow up could hardly be imagined. Bob was born in the tiny village of Rhoden Hall, high up in St Ann's Dry Harbour Mountains, about fifteen kilometres from the sea, on 6 February 1945. He was named Robert Nesta Marley, and his parents were Cedella Booker, a

Cedella with Bob

nineteen-year-old peasant woman, and Norval Sinclair Marley, a white man who was much older than Cedella, fifty-five or fifty-six.

Cedella and Norval married in 1944, but by the time Bob was born Norval had left his wife and set up house on his own in Kingston. Norval's parents disapproved of him marrying a poor black woman, and they told him they would not leave him any money when they died if he carried on living with Cedella. Norval, who was already quite old and worried about what would become of him when he was no longer able to work, gave in to the demands of his parents.

If Norval seems now to have been a rather weak and cowardly man, Bob's young mother was an altogether stronger and more resourceful person. She was determined to bring up her son as well as she possibly could, so she opened up a little grocery shop in Rhoden

13

Hall, selling simple foodstuffs like rice, fruit and vegetables. The shop never made much money, but it enabled Cedella and Bob to survive without Norval — which was just as well, since Norval hardly ever came to visit his wife and son. Later, when Bob was a famous singer, journalists often asked him about his father, but all Bob could remember was that he had a red face and smoked a pipe.

With Norval gone, Bob turned to Cedella's father, Omeriah Malcolm, who lived nearby. In Jamaica, old people hardly ever have to go and live in special retirement homes with other people of their own age, but carry on living with or near their children. This is much nicer for the old people, and good for the younger members of the family too, who can benefit from the things the old people have learned during their lives. Omeriah had a big influence on the way Cedella brought Bob up, and that influence was to stay with Bob all his life.

A small farmer, Omeriah was widely respected in Rhoden Hall for his skills as a 'myalman'. (A myalman is someone who is believed to be able to counter witchcraft, which Jamaicans call 'obeah', and to heal sick people with herbal or folk medicines.) Because Jamaica is not as rich as some Western countries, it does not have as many doctors and hospitals as it needs, and many of the poorest people cannot afford to pay for medicines in chemist shops. So a myalman like Omeriah, with his cheap but effective cures made from plants and roots, is a highly valued member of the community in which he lives.

Omeriah had been taught the secrets of a myalman by his father, who was descended from the slaves who were taken to Jamaica from Ghana (on the west coast of Africa). In turn he handed the knowledge down to his own children. Cedella taught Bob to respect their ancient healing skills, and the myalman's belief in spirits and ghosts. Later, when Bob began writing songs and making records, he often referred to myalman ideas in his lyrics.

But that was much later. First Bob had to go to school like other children, and move from peaceful St Ann to the dirty and violent streets of Trenchtown, the most notorious slum in Kingston.

Trenchtown

3 Concrete Jungle

When Bob was five years old, he started going to Stepney School, with all the other children in Rhoden Hall. Each morning, before he set off for classes, he helped Cedella to tidy up the shop and arrange displays of fruit and vegetables on tables outside the front door. He then set out on the long walk to school. He used to take a picnic lunch of sweet potato or banana, and a drink of coconut milk, which he ate in the playground during his lunch-break. All the children brought picnic lunches because Stepney School was too small to have its own kitchen or dinner-helpers. After school, he would help his mother in the shop again, or perhaps give Omeriah a hand herding his goats into their pens for the night. Then, when it was supper time, Bob and Cedella used to join Omeriah for a dish of rice and beans, mixed with some chicken or fish if Cedella had earned enough money in the shop that day. There was no electric light or television, so when it was dark Bob went to bed.

Bob enjoyed Stepney School, and he liked helping his mother and grandfather in their work. He would probably have carried on living in Rhoden Hall for many years if Norval had not suddenly intervened.

Bob helping Cedella

When Bob was six, Norval wrote to Cedella urging her to send Bob to school in Kingston. He would receive a better education there, wrote Norval, because the schools were bigger, had more teachers and a better range of textbooks and teaching aids. Norval said that Bob could live with a woman he knew called Miss Grey.

Cedella did not really want to send Bob to Kingston, but she did want him to have the best education possible. She and Omeriah discussed Norval's suggestion many times, and eventually she wrote to Norval agreeing to send Bob away. So one morning, Bob was put on the 'bungo' (country bumpkin) bus from Rhoden Hall to Kingston. As there were hardly any trains in Jamaica, and only the richest people had cars, practically everybody travelled on the bungo buses. Bob had to squeeze in amongst a crowd of market

The 'bungo' bus

women going to Kingston for the day, who were carrying great baskets of fruit and vegetables, and even had goats and chickens in tow. The journey to Kingston took several hours, and a tired Bob was met at the bus station by Norval, who took him straight to Miss Grey's house in a pony trap.

Miss Grey lived in Trenchtown, and the contrast between that area and Rhoden Hall must have made poor Bob think he had moved to another planet! Few of the houses had gardens, there were hardly any trees in the streets, and there was litter scattered all over the place (because most of the people in Trenchtown were so poor that they could not afford to buy things like dustbins). The houses were different too — in Rhoden Hall they were small, but they were still nice, and were made out of local wood and stone and painted in bright, cheerful colours. In Trenchtown, on the other hand, the houses were mean and rickety affairs made out of old sheets of corrugated iron that had been collected from rubbish dumps. Some of them were even made out of flattened cardboard boxes.

Bob spent a year living with Miss Grey, and then Cedella decided that, better schools or not, she wanted him to leave Kingston and come back to live at home again. Education, she realised, was not only a matter of big schools with smart libraries, but had a lot to do with where you lived and who you lived with. Miss Grey was pleasant enough, but Norval had never gone to visit his son, and Cedella decided that Bob would be better off amongst his family and the happy people of Rhoden Hall.

4 The Birth of the Wailers

Bob carried on attending Stepney School until 1955 when he was ten years old. Then Cedella decided that she would take him to Kingston herself, where she had been offered a cheap flat on a government housing estate in Trenchtown. The grocery shop in Rhoden Hall was no longer making enough money to support Cedella and a growing boy like Bob, and for all its disadvantages, living in Trenchtown did at least mean that Cedella would be able to find a better paid job in Kingston. She also thought that Bob was now old enough to benefit from the more advanced Kingston schools, and that living in Kingston would make it easier for him to find a job when the time came for him to leave school.

One of Bob's best friends in his new home was a boy called Bunny Livingston, who was the same age as him and lived next door. The two boys went to the same school and played together in the evenings and at weekends. They grew so close over the next few years that many people who saw them together thought that they must be brothers. When they were about fourteen, Bob and Bunny started going to the 'blues dances' that were held in Kingston on Friday and Saturday nights.

A blues dance

At a blues dance a disc jockey sets up his record player in a local dance hall and plays records for anyone who can afford to pay a few pence to get in. Most people in Jamaica were too poor to own record players, especially in Trenchtown, so the blues dances were very popular.

It was because of these dances that Bob first thought about becoming a singer. He was an ambitious boy, who wanted to do well in life, and he thought that making records and giving concerts would be a quick and easy way to make enough money to live in a comfortable house away from the slums of Trenchtown. Back in the 1950s (and even today), it was difficult for a young boy or girl in the Kingston slums to find a well paid job, and music (or sport) was one of the few opportunities open to them. Becoming a successful singer or athlete had nothing to do with what sort of family you came from, and a talented working class youngster could compete on equal terms with someone from a wealthier background. Bob was good at football, which he and Bunny often played in the street, but making records seemed a more exciting and less strenuous way of life.

So in 1960, when they were both about fifteen, Bob and Bunny formed a group with two of their friends, Peter Tosh and Rita Anderson. They called themselves the Wailin' Wailers, and started out by copying the records they heard disc jockeys playing at the blues dances. After a year or so they began to write their own songs, and it was then that the Wailin' Wailers were asked to play at clubs in and around Trenchtown. There was no real leader of the group then, although

Writing a song

Bob wrote most of the songs, and the four Wailin' Wailers shared the singing and guitar-playing.

Even in these early days, there was something special about the Wailin' Wailers that set them apart from the other groups in the neighbourhood. For a start, they had a raw energy and excitement that few other groups could rival. Also, while other groups sang about fast cars and expensive night clubs, the Wailin' Wailers sang about things the people of Trenchtown could really understand — bad housing, hard work and poor wages. Bob was already writing the sort of songs that would make him a worldwide superstar; protest songs that concerned themselves with the real world rather than fairy tales of fantasy and wishful thinking.

The Wailin' Wailers won more and more fans, and it was not long before the record companies in Kingston began to hear about the group. Talent scouts from various labels started coming to dances to hear the band play, and in 1963 one of the leading companies in the city, *Studio One*, offered the group the chance to make their first record, Simmer Down. Written by Bob, the lyrics talked about the gang fights that were making Trenchtown a dangerous place in which to live, and urged the rival gangs to make peace with each other (a theme of many of Bob's later songs as well). Simmer Down was an immediate hit in the Trenchtown area, and was followed by hits with songs like Lonesome Feelings, Train To Skaville, and Love And Affection. By 1964 the Wailin' Wailers were popular not just in Trenchtown but all over Kingston. People in country areas of Jamaica were also beginning to follow the group, thanks to the disc jockeys who played their records at blues dances in village halls and squares throughout the island.

By the time Christmas 1964 arrived, Bob must have thought that his dreams of making a quick and easy fortune out of music were about to come true. Things were going so well for the Wailin' Wailers that it seemed nothing could stop them. In fact, he was about to learn some harsh truths about the way the music business in Jamaica was organised, and to appreciate that fortune did not always follow fame.

A talent scout

5 Rebel Music

Bob thought that once the Wailin' Wailers began to make hit records they would quickly earn enough money to be able to live in a nicer place than Trenchtown. After all, he had seen famous musicians like the Skatalites (then the most popular group in Jamaica) walking around town dressed in expensive foreign clothes and driving flashy cars. What he did not realise was that those clothes were often the only things the musicians owned apart from their instruments — and that the cars usually belonged to the businessmen who owned the record companies. Even the most famous Jamaican musicians were really only paid pocket money for each record they played on, and even if their records were number one hits they were still not given any extra money. Of course, musicians like the Skatalites liked to pretend they were wealthy people, so younger musicians felt sure that they too were going to be rich.

In their first two years with *Studio One*, the Wailin' Wailers made a new single almost every month. Many of these were hits, but despite this the group still had to struggle to pay for enough food for one good meal a day. They were barely earning sufficient money to survive in Trenchtown, let alone to move to a more attractive part of town. So when, towards the end of 1965, Cedella gave Bob enough money to travel to America, he was delighted. Maybe in America, the fabled land of opportunity, he would be able to find a way to make the Wailin' Wailers earn the money they deserved.

Before Bob left Jamaica, he and Rita decided to get married. As they had spent more and more time singing together, the pair had gradually fallen in love. For the wedding Bob wore his smartest stage suit and Rita her prettiest party dress. Peter and Bunny were witnesses. Bob was just twenty-one and Rita was nineteen.

Bob arrived in America full of excitement, but soon decided that he hated the country and its way of life. Everybody always seemed to be in a rush, and after Jamaica the weather was colder than he had ever dreamed possible. On top of all this, the American army sent him a letter saying he would have to become a soldier if he carried on living in the country. At that time all young American men had to spend two or three years learning to be soldiers. Bob detested guns and killing, and hated the idea of having to become a soldier. He returned to Jamaica before his call-up papers arrived.

He came back to Trenchtown determined to put even more effort into becoming a successful and wealthy musician. The businessmen at the record companies might be mean, but if the Wailin' Wailers kept trying, Bob was certain that somehow their fortunes would improve. Rita was thrilled to have her husband back with her, and Peter and Bunny were pleased too; while

Rehearsing with Joe Higgs

Bob was away they had realised more than before just how important his singing was to the group, and how inspired and original his songwriting really was.

The Wailers — who had now dropped the word 'Wailin'' from their name — began to spend many of their afternoons rehearsing in a backyard belonging to their old friend and neighbour Joe Higgs. Joe was a singer and composer who was a legend in Trenchtown; a real genius, who turned his back on fame and preferred to live in poverty rather than make lots of money for the greedy men who ran the record companies. Joe saw that the Wailers had a special talent like his own, and was happy to teach them to become even better and more professional. Under his guidance, the Wailers recorded hit after hit in 1967 and 1968. Some of these records are still favourites with reggae fans today — songs like, Who Feels It Knows It, Dream Land and Rasta Put It On.

But when it came to money it was the same old story. The Wailers were having hits and their fans were becoming more and more numerous, but the group was still poor and hungry. Bob realised that things would never improve unless the group could get hits in bigger and richer countries like Britain and America. The problem was, how were they going to get those hits? *Studio One* only sold a few records outside Jamaica, and none of the Wailers knew anybody who could help them make records for a big foreign company. Then a chance meeting with a successful American singer called Johnny Nash, who was visiting Jamaica, looked like changing their luck.

6 Rasta Man Chant

Johnny Nash heard the Wailers at a club he went to one night in Kingston, and was so impressed by what he heard, and by the reactions of the other people in the audience, that he spoke to the group and suggested that they should help each other. In return for Bob writing songs for him, Nash said that he would play the Wailers' records to big record companies in America, who might be interested in putting the records on sale in America and Europe. If this happened, and the records sold well, the Wailers would soon be very rich indeed. While a record could be a hit in Jamaica by selling only a few thousand copies, a hit in America meant a group had sold anywhere between a quarter of a million and a million records. Even if the group only made a few pence on every copy they sold, that would add up to a huge amount of money.

Nash did play the Wailers' records to record companies in America, but to start with none of them thought it worth putting the records on sale in American shops. They believed that reggae could only ever be popular in Jamaica, and that Americans would always prefer rock and roll, rhythm and blues, or British groups like the Beatles and the Rolling Stones.

Nash proved these people wrong, however, by recording some of Bob's songs himself, and one of these, Stir It Up, was a big hit both in America and Britain (where it reached number twelve in the charts).

Meanwhile, in 1969, Bob and the other Wailers met a Jamaican record producer called Lee Perry, who started recording the Wailers for his own *Upsetter* label. Perry was the ideal producer for the Wailers because he had the same ideas about reggae that they did. Like them, Perry preferred to make songs about subjects the poor people in Jamaica felt were real, for he believed that songs which protested about slums and poverty would sell many more copies than those that pretended that everything was alright. Perry was also an excellent songwriter himself, and his partnership with the group, which lasted until 1972, resulted in some of the finest records the Wailers ever made. Songs like Small Axe, African Herbsman, Soul Rebel and Duppy Conqueror, all produced by Perry, are still favourites with reggae fans today, some fifteen or so years after they were first released.

During their partnership with Perry, Bob and the

other Wailers became deeply involved with the Rastafarian movement which was then being adopted by many people in Jamaica — particularly by young people in the slums who called themselves 'sufferers'. Rastafarianism, a semi-religious and semi-political movement, first began around 1930. It claimed that Jamaica could never be the real home of the black people who lived there; and that their true home was Africa, from where their ancestors had been taken in slavery centuries before. Rastafarian philosophy had grown out of the writings and speeches of many black thinkers, the most important of whom were Haile Selassie (the Emperor of Ethiopia, in north-eastern Africa, from 1930 to 1974), and Marcus Garvey (a Jamaican politician, born like Bob in the St Ann area of the island, who had formed the *Universal Negro Improvement Association* in 1917).

Rastafarianism offered answers and advice to poor black people who no longer believed that the established political parties or churches wanted to help them. Bob and the Wailers became enthusiastic Rastas, as did many of the people who bought their records. They grew their hair into lengthy 'dreadlocks' (Rastas believe it is wrong to cut your hair), and read a chapter of the Bible every day, as all devout Rastas are meant to. In Jamaica in the late 1960s and early 1970s, as in other parts of the world today, Rastas were often feared and misunderstood by other people in society, who looked on them as layabouts and criminals. This was partly because their dreadlocks gave them such a frightening appearance, and partly because they preferred to smoke marijuana (which they called 'herb') rather than drink alcohol. They claimed that the Bible instructed them to smoke 'the green herb', but the police said it was against the law. Many Rastas were put in jail because of this.

Bob was convinced that Rastafarianism was the real answer to the problems that faced black people in Jamaica and elsewhere, and despite the disapproval of policemen and politicians he continued to sing about the faith throughout his life. Almost all the songs he wrote and recorded from 1969 onwards included some Rastafarian ideas, and Rastafarianism and the Wailers grew hand in hand. The more Bob publicised the faith, the more members of his audience called themselves Rastas; and the more Rastas there were in his audience, the more Bob was encouraged to carry on singing and talking about his beliefs.

Rastafarians

7 Catch a Fire

When the Johnny Nash recording of Stir It Up climbed the pop charts in Britain and America, some of the big record companies in those countries began to take a new interest in Bob and the Wailers. If Bob could write a hit song for Johnny Nash, they thought to themselves, perhaps he could have his own hits with other songs. So Bob began to have visits from representatives of these companies, who asked him if he would like to make records specially for them. Of course, Bob was very excited about this, for his ambition had always been to sell records not just in Jamaica but all over the world. At the same time, however, he knew that most British and American record companies did not really understand or even like reggae, and so he reluctantly turned down the various offers of recording contracts that were made to him.

Then, towards the end of 1971, Bob finally met the record company which he believed was the right one for him. It was called *Island*, and though it was based in London it was owned by a white Jamaican named Chris Blackwell, and had been specialising in Jamaican music since the early 1960s. Blackwell had started *Island* all on his own, selling his records to record shops himself. He had such a good ear for a hit that in a few years *Island* had grown into a large and very successful company. Bob believed that Blackwell's sure touch for hits, combined with his real knowledge and love of reggae, meant that *Island* was the right company for the Wailers to record with. Blackwell for his part was delighted with the Wailers. He had long believed that reggae could be successful outside Jamaica, and once he had heard the Wailers he was sure he had found the group he was looking for.

Meeting Chris Blackwell, London 1972

So in 1972 the Wailers came over to London to record their first album for *Island*, Catch A Fire. In the past, whenever they had made a record, they had been forced to do things in a great hurry, because it cost a lot of money to hire recording studios and their Jamaican producers could only afford to hire one for a few hours at a time. Most of the Wailers' singles had been recorded

Photographic session for record covers

within two or three hours, for instance, while it was quite usual for British or American rock groups to spend weeks or even months in the studios on one song, getting their sound and playing absolutely perfect.

But when the Wailers arrived in London, Blackwell told them that they could spend as much time as they needed in the studio. He said he wanted the album to be the best record *Island* had ever released. He knew that if *Island* were to make a lot of money from selling it, then the company would first have to spend a lot of money making it. Everything, from the sound in the grooves to the photographs on the cover, had to be the best that money could buy.

The obvious faith Chris Blackwell had in the Wailers convinced Bob that the group had been right to sign a contract with *Island*. The two men also agreed on the need to make Catch A Fire attractive to British rock fans, most of whom found reggae too strange and different to enjoy. So a top American rock guitarist called Wayne Perkins was flown into London to add solos to the album. Bob and Blackwell believed that the combination of the Wailers' rootsy reggae and Perkins' catchy guitar solos would make Catch A Fire a big seller with both Jamaican reggae fans and the more adventurous British rock fans.

When Catch A Fire was finally released, in early 1973, the belief Bob and Blackwell had in the music was quickly justified. Critics praised the album as one of the most exciting they had ever heard, and thousands of rock fans who had never previously had any interest in reggae rushed out to buy copies at their local record shops. At the same time, the roots reggae audience loved Catch A Fire too, and Bob was delighted that he had kept his old fans happy whilst winning lots of new ones.

By the end of 1973, Bob and the Wailers had finally realised their biggest ambition — they were recording stars on an international scale. Catch A Fire had been followed by a second *Island* album, Burnin', and American rock fans had followed their British counterparts by becoming converts to the Wailers and reggae music. Everything, indeed, seemed to be going perfectly — but, underneath the surface, trouble was brewing within the Wailers and before the next year was out, some major changes were to affect the group.

8   Roots and Branches

Anyone following the rise of the Wailers in the pop charts in 1973 and 1974 would probably have thought that Bob, Peter, Bunny and Rita were delighted with the way things were going for them. The contract with *Island*, the success of Catch A Fire and Burnin', and the conquests of Britain and America, read like the sort of story dreams are made of. Surely, then, everyone in the Wailers would be happy and getting along together well? This, however, was not the case. Although Bob and Rita were pleased with the way the Wailers' career was progressing, Peter and Bunny were growing increasingly unhappy.

The trouble was that people were now beginning to talk about Bob Marley *and* the Wailers, and it was that '*and*' which annoyed Peter and Bunny. True, Bob did sing most of the lead vocals in the group, and he did write more Wailers' songs than anyone else, but Peter and Bunny's feelings were hurt when critics and disc jockeys began talking about Bob as though he was the only Wailer of importance. When the Wailin' Wailers had started, there had been no leader and every member had been regarded as equally important. But as 1974 progressed, Peter and Bunny began to feel that

Bob, Peter, and Bunny talking about the future of the group

all anyone wanted them to do was to sing background vocals to Bob's lead vocals on Bob's own songs.

Peter and Bunny did not sulk about this, however; instead they talked to Bob, explaining how they felt. Bob understood their annoyance, and whenever he was interviewed for the newspapers he emphasised the key roles played by Peter and Bunny. But the critics were unimpressed — they knew Bob was the lead singer of the group and they knew he wrote most of the songs. So surely he must be the most important Wailer? And in a sense, of course, the critics were right, despite the loyal denials made by Bob himself.

Eventually, towards the end of 1974, Peter and Bunny separately told Bob and Rita that they were leaving the Wailers. Both men had decided to pursue solo careers — and this they continue to do today. Yet all four Wailers remained close friends, and for a while Bunny even continued to release his records on *Island*.

While the question of Peter and Bunny's place in the Wailers was being settled, the group had been unable to set about recording a follow-up album to Burnin'. The record was finally released (without Peter and Bunny, of course) in 1975. Titled Natty Dread, it was a huge success in Britain, and when Bob and the Wailers toured the country that year they were met with excited, standing-room only audiences wherever they played. A fourth album, Live, was recorded at the Lyceum Ballroom in London on the tour, and when one of the songs, No Woman No Cry, was released as a single it gave Bob his first Top Twenty hit. There really was no stopping the Wailers now, with Peter and Bunny or without them.

9 So Much Trouble in the World

When a pop musician becomes very famous, his or her fans expect their heroes to provide answers to problems that are troubling them. How to stop war for example or how to help starving people grow enough food to eat. Sometimes it is very unfair to expect a pop musician to give the solutions to such problems, because there is a great difference between writing good and interesting songs and being able to properly understand political or economic questions.

By the time the Live album and No Woman No Cry single were rocketing up the charts, Bob was looked on by his fans — and by the critics who wrote about him in the newspapers — almost as a politician instead of

Bob reading about world politics

simply the leader of the Wailers. Up to a point he enjoyed this, for his songs were frequently about political subjects, like slavery or racial discrimination, and as a Rasta he believed he did know the answer to many problems better than the politicians themselves. So when critics asked him to talk about political subjects, he usually agreed. But, he would also emphasise that although he had strong ideas about politics, he never wanted to be a real politician himself.

Unfortunately for Bob, many of the politicians in Jamaica did not believe him when he said he didn't want to be a politician himself. They thought that if they offered him enough money, or some other gift like a free house by the sea or a new Rolls Royce car, he would tell his fans to vote for the party or politician who had given him the present. The politicians kept trying to make him agree to such an arrangement, because they knew that if he told his fans to vote for a certain person then most of them probably would.

Because Bob kept saying no to these offers of money or other bribes, the politicians grew very angry with him. In 1976, some of them actually tried to assassinate him at his home in Kingston. Bob and the rest of the Wailers were sitting in the living-room having a meal when suddenly a group of men burst in firing machine guns. One of the bullets wounded Bob in his arm, and he would almost certainly have been killed if the manager of the Wailers, Don Taylor, had not been standing between him and the gunmen. Don Taylor was hit by the bullets that were meant for Bob and was very nearly killed.

43

Assassination attempt

Of course, this was a terrifying experience for Bob and the others. Like anybody else, they wanted to find somewhere safe and hide there until the gunmen had been caught and sent to prison. But the very next day the Wailers were meant to be playing at a big open-air concert called the Peace Treaty Festival, which was being organised to try to stop political gangwar and murders. Bob thought that if the Wailers cancelled their appearance it would be a victory for the gunmen and political thugs, and so, very bravely, the group did appear on stage. Bob led the Wailers through a stirring

The Peace Treaty Festival, 1976

performance, which included some of the songs he had written about the stupidity of guns and violence, and the need for peace and understanding in the world.

The Peace Treaty Festival was a huge successs, and no further attempt was made on Bob's life, but within hours of the concert ending he caught a plane to Miami, a city on the south-east coast of America. He decided it would be safer for him to stay there until the men who had tried to murder him had been caught by the police. But the gunmen never were caught, and because of this he spent over a year in Miami. The assassination attempt had taken place just before Christmas 1976, and Bob did not return to Jamaica until the spring of 1978. The event which persuaded him to return home was another open air concert which was supposed to bring peace to Jamaican political life — the One Love Peace Concert.

The Peace Concert was being organised by two of the gangleaders who had been responsible for many of the

Persuading Michael Manley and Edward Seaga to shake hands

political assassinations in Jamaica. The two men had now decided to stop fighting and killing, and the concert was meant to tell everybody that a new time of peace and understanding had come to Jamaica. Naturally, Bob was delighted by this news and agreed that both he and the Wailers would play at the concert. When the Wailers were on stage, Bob persuaded Jamaica's two leading politicians — Michael Manley (then Prime Minister) and Edward Seaga (then Leader of the Opposition) — to join the group and shake hands in front of the audience. It was a tremendous moment, and proved once and for all that Bob was no ordinary pop star.

The success of the One Love Peace Concert inspired a new burst of creative energy in Bob. Refreshed from his enforced holiday in Miami, he set about recording some of the most powerful music the Wailers had ever made, starting with the remarkable Survival album in 1979. For many people, Survival remains the most exciting album the Wailers ever made, and it included some of Bob's finest songs — Ambush (which told of an attempted assassination), Africa Unite (where Bob urged African countries to stop fighting each other and live together in peace), and One Drop (a moving song of encouragement to suffering people all over the world). Bob also made a number of important concert tours with the Wailers, travelling to Kenya, Ethiopia, Zimbabwe, Japan, Australia, Britain and America.

By the end of 1979, Bob and the Wailers had reached a position of popularity around the world which could only be compared with that of the Beatles in the 1960s, or perhaps Michael Jackson in the 1980s. Then, just when Bob was riding so high that it seemed nothing could ever stop him, tragedy struck and everything began to change.

10 Exodus

Back in 1977, when Bob was playing football with some friends, he had injured one of his toes so badly that he had had to go to hospital to see a doctor. When the doctor examined Bob's foot, he discovered that Bob had a cancerous growth on the injured toe. Bob was told that he should have the toe amputated in order to stop the cancer spreading, but he refused, believing that he could cure himself through herbal medicine and other natural remedies. For a while it looked as though he was going to be alright, but towards the end

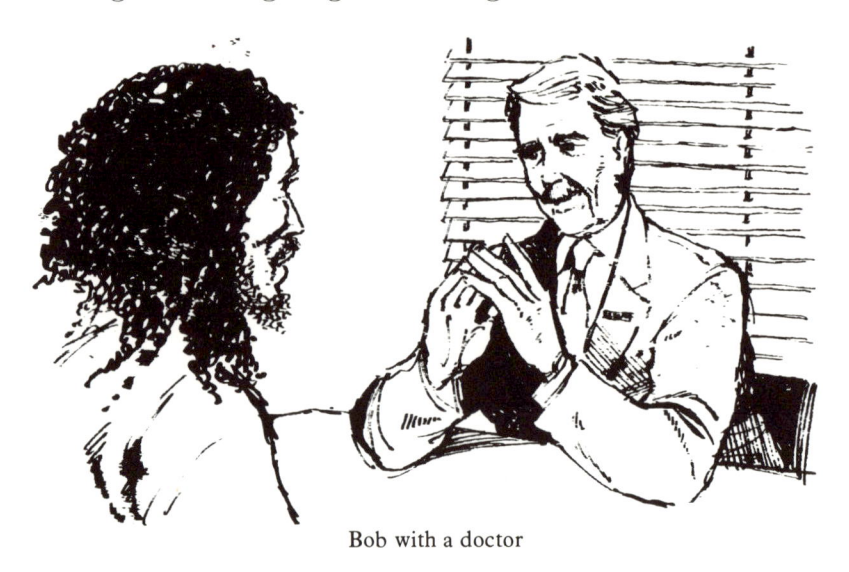

Bob with a doctor

Bob collapses on tour

of 1980 he discovered that the cancer had spread from his toe throughout his body.

1980 began well enough, with a new album being released and Bob and the Wailers starting an ambitious world tour that was to take them through fifteen countries over a period of nine months. The tour opened in Gabon in West Africa in January and was to end in the USA in September. After a concert in New York shortly before the tour was due to end, Bob collapsed. At first the doctors thought he was simply suffering from exhaustion after such a long tour. But when they learnt that he had had treatment for a cancerous toe three years earlier, they made further tests and found that the cancer had spread.

The doctors in New York believed that Bob was so ill

Bob ill in hospital

Bob in Switzerland

that little could be done to save his life. But Bob, a fighter to the last, disagreed — and for a while it seemed that he was right and that a miracle would happen. He went to a special hospital in Switzerland and for a few months seemed to be getting better. But tragically, the recovery was only temporary, and in the spring of 1981 he decided to travel back to Jamaica, to see his home for the last time. He died on 11 May 1981 in Miami, on the last leg of his journey.

When Bob died, reggae fans all over the world went into mourning, with those in Jamaica particularly grief-stricken. For many Jamaicans, Bob Marley was much more than a successful pop star — he was a symbol of national pride and hope, someone who represented Jamaican ability and ambition. The Jamaican government was well aware of the love the people had for Bob, and shortly before he died they awarded him the Order Of Merit. Now he was dead the government decided to give him the sort of elaborate state funeral normally reserved for prime ministers, or kings and queens.

   The day before the funeral, Bob's body lay in state at the National Arena, a massive indoor sports arena that had been built for the Commonwealth Games years before. For hours, his fans queued to pay their last respects at the side of his coffin. On Thursday 21 May the funeral service itself took place — first a private affair for Bob's family and close friends, then a public ceremony at the National Arena. Big as it was, the Arena was too small to hold all Bob's fans, thousands of whom gathered outside the doors, singing songs that Bob had made famous, and saying prayers. Finally, Bob's body was taken by car out of Kingston and back to

The funeral

his birthplace at Rhoden Hall, where it was to be buried. All along the route people gathered to bid Bob farewell, and at Rhoden Hall thousands more were waiting. The grave at Rhoden Hall was officially declared a Jamaican national shrine, and Kingston Washington Boulevard, one of the city's most important roads, was renamed Bob Marley Boulevard. The government also announced that a special statue of Bob would be erected in a new National Heroes Park.

There were tributes of another kind too, as reggae singers all over the world released records that praised Bob and his career in music. Some of these records were sincere, sung by friends of Bob who genuinely meant what they sang. But others, sadly, were simply greedy attempts to make some money out of Bob's death.

When a star as important and popular as Bob dies, it is not only other singers who try to cash in on the event — usually his or her record company do the same, rushing to release lots of records. Often these records are inferior ones, that would never have been made public if the singer had not died. *Island Records*, to their credit, never did this with Bob, and it was a full two years after his death before they released another of his records. It was called Confrontation, and was a collection of songs Bob had recorded towards the end of his life. It was tremendously successful, as was Legend, released in 1984.

Today, the records Bob made remain as popular with reggae fans as they were when they first came out, and are almost certain to remain so for years to come. As with the late Elvis Presley or John Lennon, Bob was such a musical giant in his own lifetime that his fans remain just as loyal and enthusiastic after his death. And while other singers have emerged from Jamaica since he died, no one has, as yet, come along to take the place he occupied.

Fans still buying records

The Marley children

Bob's memory lives on in other ways too. Under the guidance of Rita, Bob's children have begun a recording career. Calling themselves the Melody Makers, the four children — Sharon, Cedella, Ziggy and Stevie — have built up a growing audience amongst reggae fans, and other children in countries all across the world.

There is little danger of the music of Bob Marley being forgotten in the foreseeable future. As long as there are hungry or badly treated people in the world, there will always be an audience for his songs.